BARRON'S STUDIES IN AMERICAN LITERATURE

J. D. SALINGER:
THE CATCHER IN THE RYE

by
RICHARD LETTIS
C. W. Post College
Long Island University

BARRON'S EDUCATIONAL SERIES, INC.
GREAT NECK, NEW YORK

WARNER MEMORIAL LIBRARY
EASTERN COLLEGE
ST. DAVIDS, PA. 19087

© 1964 by Barron's Educational Series, Inc.
343 GREAT NECK ROAD
GREAT NECK, NEW YORK

All rights are strictly reserved.
Todos Derechos Reservados.
No part of this book may be reproduced in any
form, by mimeograph or any other means, without
express permission in writing from the publisher.

Library of Congress Catalog Card No. 63-17168

PRINTED IN THE UNITED STATES OF AMERICA

```
PS 3537 .A426 C33
Lettis, Richard.
J. D. Salinger: The catcher
  in the rye
```

ACKNOWLEDGMENTS

I gratefully acknowledge the assistance given by Professor William E. Morris of Ohio University in preparing this text. Professor Morris made contributions to the chapter questions, the general questions, the critical selections, and the bibliography.

I also wish to express my thanks to the following people for assistance: Mrs. Avis M. Duckworth, Director of the South Huntington Public Library, for tireless assistance in finding Salinger criticism; to Priscilla Lettis, wife, for keeping the children out of my study.

Contents

INTRODUCTION	vii
THE AUTHOR	1
HOLDEN CAULFIELD	3
QUESTIONS FOR STUDY AND DISCUSSION	19
GENERAL QUESTIONS	37
CRITICAL COMMENTS	40
A SALINGER BIBLIOGRAPHY	44

Introduction

The purpose of this text is to assist you in your study of *The Catcher in the Rye*. To this end it will provide you with the following materials: 1) a biographical sketch of the author, J. D. Salinger; 2) a look at some of the ideas of the novel through a brief discussion of its protagonist, Holden Caulfield; 3) questions about incidents and details in the novel, and about its larger concepts; 4) quotations and paraphrases of important criticism dealing with *The Catcher in the Rye*; 5) a bibliography of Salinger's fiction and of criticism of it.

The above material should not be thought of as "covering" *The Catcher in the Rye* completely, any more than your class discussions or your own study will exhaust the novel. A truly worthwhile novel is never finished; one goes back again and again to mine it, and discovers as he does so that he has opened up two new veins of ore for each one that he has worked out. Therefore you will find much to talk about with your instructor, and much more to write about if you go on to write an essay or research paper on *The Catcher*. This text hopes only to help you to begin, for it has been the experience of its author that the beginning is the most difficult for those who try to talk about what they have read. "I have read it," they say. "Now what? It's just a story about a boy, and I liked it (or didn't like it). What else is there to say?"

It is hoped that the materials mentioned above will help you to find something else that you want to say. The biography will not prove as useful as those provided in other texts of this series, for Mr. Salinger is a reticent man, and will not tell us much about himself. Still, you will want to know the few facts that are available, and you may find your interest in Holden Caulfield increasing when you learn that in at least some ways he is autobiographical. Then you will go on to read an approach to Holden Caulfield, which may be of use to you in several ways. If you have not considered this approach before, and if it convinces you, you will want to read the novel again with this new perspective in mind, looking for evidence that will support your reading. If you are not convinced, you will try to marshal arguments against this approach to Holden. But whether you decide to defend, attack, or modify the ideas you encounter, in the end you will have a better understanding of Holden, of the world as he sees it, and of the world as you think his creator wants you to see it.

The questions are designed to call your attention to more specific problems. Those which deal with the chapters of the novel will concentrate on particulars: how does Salinger develop character through dress, action, thought, word? How does he present a scene, work up a climax, end a chapter? How selective is he—what kinds of details does he include, and what does he omit? Does he employ symbols? And so on. Some of these questions will be easy; as you reread the passages to which they direct you, you will be able to provide a full and satisfactory answer. Others will be more difficult; you will need the help of classmates and the instructor to find an answer. And there may be some for which no answer can be found by anybody, for not even the most percipient reader can solve all the problems a good novel provides. Indeed, that is part of the pleasure: everyone tries, but no one can be certain that his is the right answer (though there are ways of deciding which is the better answer). Even the "experts" often find themselves in fundamental disagreement. The quotations provided in the next section will illustrate this, and you will have the opportunity to decide which quotations are valid criticism of *The*

Catcher and which are not. When you have read these through perhaps you will want to find some more opinions to agree and disagree with, so that your command of Holden and his story may become still more complete. If so, you will turn to the bibliography of Salinger criticism which is provided at the end of the text. You will also find a list of Salinger's writings, for if you wish to read more about him you will doubtless also want to read more of him.

In short, we are suggesting that *The Catcher in the Rye* will catch you. If it does, you stand with the majority. Ten years after its publication on July 16, 1951, the novel had sold over 1,500,000 copies, most of them to high school and college students; it continues to sell 250,000 copies a year. At present the paperback edition (New American Library, 1953) is the best seller, but the novel is still available in three hard cover editions (Little, Brown & Co., 1951—the original publishers; Grosset and Dunlap, 1952; Modern Library, 1958). *The Catcher* has met with similar success abroad, despite the problems of translating Holden's colloquial speech. Undoubtedly we cannot account for the popularity of the novel solely in terms of its artistic worth, for quality is not always an important selling feature. Perhaps Robert Gutwillig, in his "Everybody's Caught 'The Catcher in the Rye'" (see bibliography), has best defined for us the cause of our continuing interest:

> What was it about the novel that struck Americans so squarely ten years ago and continues to hit the mark still? Primarily it was, I think, the shock and thrill of recognition. Many of my friends and this writer himself identified completely with Holden. I went to a school much like Pencey Prep. One of my friends had a younger brother like Allie, who had died, another an older brother like D. B., still another a younger sister like Phoebe. After reading the novel, several of us went out and bought ourselves red caps with earflaps, and we all took to calling each other "Ace" and "Prince."

But the undoubted appeal of *The Catcher in the Rye* to its own generation is not sufficient basis for the final evaluation of its worth. This can only be done by the individual decisions of the thousands who read it and form opinions about it.

What is your opinion? If you have one, the pages of this text may challenge you to defend or modify it. If you haven't, these pages may help you to acquire one. After all, *The Catcher in the Rye* was written for you: it's your opinion that counts.

Richard Lettis

HUNTINGTON STATION, N. Y.
MARCH, 1964

The Author

On the dust-jacket of his second novel, *Franny and Zooey*, J. D. Salinger wrote:

> It is my rather subversive opinion that a writer's feelings of anonymity-obscurity are the second-most valuable property on loan to him during his working years. My wife has asked me to add, however, in a single explosion of candor, that I live in Westport with my dog.

Mr. Salinger thus aligns himself with a small group of contemporary writers (the late William Faulkner was the most prominent member) who resist the trend toward pedestal-standing and grandstanding in the Hemingway tradition. Students of Mr. Salinger's work must respect his wishes, however reluctantly. But we present here such information as has already been made public through *Who's Who*, *Twentieth Century Authors: First Supplement*, and the editors of magazines which have published his short stories. We lean too on the most complete gathering of biographical information to date—John Skow's "Sonny; An Introduction," which appeared in *Time*, September 15, 1961. (This information was gathered by several reporters, including Robert Jones, Martha Murphy McDowell, Art Seidenbaum, and William Smith.)

Jerome David Salinger was born in 1919 in New York City, where he spent his childhood. He attended public school, McBurney School, and Valley Forge Military Academy in Pennsylvania; later he studied at three colleges, but did not take a degree. Before the Second World War he traveled in Europe, where he later served in the U. S. Army (1942-1946), participating in five combat campaigns as a staff sergeant in the Fourth Infantry Division.

Mr. Salinger began writing at the age of fifteen, and published his first short story ("The Young Folks") in *Story* magazine in 1940. Since then he has published extensively in such magazines as *Harper's*, *The Saturday Evening Post*, *Esquire*, *Cosmopolitan*, and *The New Yorker* (see bibliography). "Uncle Wiggily in Connecticut" (*New Yorker*, 1948) was produced as a motion picture entitled *My Foolish Heart*. To date, in addition to *The Catcher in the Rye*, three books of Salinger's stories have appeared: *Nine Stories* (1953), *Franny and Zooey* (1961) and *Raise High the Roof Beam, Carpenters* (1963). Since the publishing of *Nine Stories*, his production has been limited to stories concerned with the Glass family: "Franny," "Raise High the Roof Beam, Carpenters," "Zooey," and "Seymour—an Introduction," all of which have appeared in *The New Yorker*. He has said that there will be "some new material soon or Soon."

At present J. D. Salinger lives in Cornish, New Hampshire, in virtual seclusion, married to the former Claire Douglas. The Salingers have two children: Matthew, born 1960, and Margaret Ann, born 1955. Henry Anatole Grunwald, in his book *Salinger, A Critical and Personal Portrait* (Harper & Brothers, 1962), adds that in school Salinger managed the fencing team, as did Holden Caulfield, that he was once an expert pool player, and that he has an interest in Oriental philosophy (witness the Glass stories). When *Harper's* published "Down at the Dinghy" Salinger added a note about himself:

> All writers—no matter how many rebellions they actively support—go to their graves half-Oliver Twist and half-Mary, Mary, Quite Contrary.

But perhaps the critic who referred to Salinger as the Greta Garbo of American Letters has labeled Salinger best of all.

Holden Caulfield

An understanding of *The Catcher in the Rye* must begin with Holden Caulfield, who is the catcher, the narrator, the protagonist—the reality of the novel. With a few possible exceptions (Phoebe?), nothing in the story is of importance except in its relationship to him. Like Stephen Dedalus in James Joyce's *A Portrait of the Artist as a Young Man*, Holden so occupies the center of attention that other characters do not really emerge from the story. In both novels the consciousness of the protagonist is the mirror in which we see his environment, and so we are able to see and know people only as one boy sees and knows them. And while Holden is a perceptive and sensitive observer, he is not a novelist; his intention is not to create living beings for us, and his opportunities for viewing and discussing the characters in his story are in most cases limited.

In *A Portrait of the Artist* the egocentricity of the protagonist is a further reason for lack of character development: Stephen is interested in others only insofar as they affect him, and so the reader never gets a chance to see them for their own sake. But this is not true of Holden, who is interested in everybody—even in a taxi driver who snarls at him, or an elevator operator who punches him. It would be better to say that he is disinterested, in the earlier sense of the word: he is concerned with understanding people, not with finding a way to use them. Therefore, though no other character in *The Catcher* is important enough to Salinger's literary purpose to be fully developed, each in a sense comes alive because he is invested with humanity through Holden's vital interest. We do not, for instance, see enough of the nuns Holden meets in a lunchroom, or of the prostitute who comes to his room, to know them fully as human beings. Some characters, such as Allie and Jane, do not even appear. But we accept them as if they had been fully developed for us because of Holden's total response to them as people—it is impossible to disbelieve in figures who are accepted so fully by a character who himself commands belief as Holden does.

In respect to character, then, the novel turns on Holden Caulfield. But what kind of a character is he? Some readers who encounter him for the first time declare that he is a pretty poor specimen of American youth. "Well, if that's a typical example of a teenager," an acquaintance of ours recently remarked, "I'm not surprised that we have such a juvenile delinquency problem." On the other hand, a scholarly study of the novel has declared that Holden "never does a wrong thing." Which judgment is more nearly correct? Obviously the first comes closer if we judge Holden by the usual standards; so considered, he never does a *right* thing. As his story opens, he has just flunked out of secondary school for the third time, and is about to run away to New York without the knowledge of his parents or the school authorities. While there, he gets drunk (permissible for adults but terrible for a boy), invites a prostitute to his hotel room, tries to pick up girls in a nightclub, insults a girlfriend, tells lies, admits to an interest in sexual perversion, calls himself an atheist and—to cut short the list of sins—ends his holiday by catching pneumonia (perhaps the greatest crime a youngster can commit is to fall ill).

Nor is this all. Though Holden is in general polite, his private comments on the adult world are at the least not respectful. And his language, the proper reader feels, is abominable, larded as it is with profanity and vulgarity to the degree that the book is often a target for those who would censor literature (in at least one case it has been banned from a college classroom). Truly, Holden is not a good boy, judged by conventional standards.

The trouble is that no perceptive reader can hold on to these standards for long in the face of Holden's obvious goodness. To begin with, we soon learn not to accept his self-accusations. He considers himself a coward—"a pacifist, if you want to know"; in one instance he dwells at some length upon his probable pusillanimity in a given situation (115f.).* But we know that, though Holden can be frightened, he is not a coward. When he fears that the virtue of Jane Gallagher is in danger, he assaults Stradlater, his physical superior. He does not flinch before the bully Maurice. But much more important than such physical courage is the moral tenacity with which he clings to his beliefs in the face of a hostile society; of this we will soon speak more fully.

Holden's sexual activities are also such as may ultimately be praised rather than blamed, though they do not conform to accepted moral codes. He is not angelic—he does not tell us that he would rather help old ladies across the street than kiss pretty young ones, as the heroes of boys' magazines commonly imply by their actions, but then Holden is a living being, not a fabricated figure set up as a model for children. While in the hotel, he admits that sexual perversion fascinates him. Few of us are equally honest, but psychiatrists tell us that such interest is common to all of us. But the point is that Holden also recognizes the ugliness of perversion, and regrets his inability to dissociate himself from it. He says, "The thing is, though, I don't *like* the idea. It stinks, if you analyze it. . . . It's really too bad that so much crumby stuff is a lot of fun sometimes." Holden dislikes things he finds in himself, but he is honest enough to admit that they are there.

* Page references are to the Modern Library Edition.

Later, Holden bargains for the services of a call girl. He tries to rationalize his physical desire by considering the experience as useful: "I figured if she was a prostitute and all, I could get in some practise on her, in case I ever get married or anything." But when this mere prostitute comes, and attempts to arouse Holden, he suddenly freezes, invents an excuse, and sends her away. He does not do so for the usual "moral" reasons—religion (in its immediate and institutional sense), or mother, or physical and mental hygiene. Nor does he refuse because the sex act disgusts him (we remember that elsewhere he has called himself a sex maniac). Indeed, Holden does not seem to know why he has rejected Sunny's advances, but as he describes his emotions we realize the true reason. First, he is embarrassed: Sunny in her slip is discomfiting instead of (as in the drugstore classics) provocative. Second, Holden is saddened; he thinks of the girl not as a creature to satisfy his desire, but as a human being—for example, as a girl buying a dress in a store where no one knows her ignoble profession—and his concern for her debased humanity first saddens, then depresses him. As in many other cases in the novel, Holden's profound ability to understand and feel for others gets in the way of his own personal enjoyment. It is difficult to find much that is bad in this.

Elsewhere Holden's sexual morality is further clarified. A little reluctantly, he admits his virginity, and attributes it, not to formal rules of good conduct, but to his concern for the girls he has known; he feels he would be taking advantage of their weakness if he had relations with them. "They tell me to stop, so I stop. I always wish I *hadn't*, after I take them home, but I keep doing it anyway." We must remember Holden's age through all this. Sex is comparatively new to him, and has even more fascination than usual because of its novelty and mysteriousness. Still, it cannot overcome his concern for people. And unlike most juveniles, he is willing to admit his inability properly to handle this dangerous new force: "Sex is something I just don't understand."

Most of Holden's other sins also pale or disappear under examination. It is true, for example, that he uses profane and obscene words. Like sex, these words are relatively new to him, and he seems to enjoy the force and vigor which they lend to his expression. But he does not use them carelessly or insultingly—not even profanely or obscenely, one might suggest. In general he applies such words to things, not to people; he rarely seems concerned with their literal meaning, but rather uses them as a kind of vague intensifier, just as we often use the word "very" in speech. When he visits his sister's school and finds an obscene expression written on a wall, he is infuriated at the thought of children seeing and being confused by it; he wants to kill the scribbler, and rubs the words away, even though he is afraid of being taken for the writer.

It is not the intention of this discussion to declare Holden free from wrong: his creator is too good an artist to make him unbelievably perfect. But if Holden has weaknesses, they are not of a kind to be judged by our usual standards, which may in general be serviceable, but which seem superficial when applied to him. We might desire to improve Holden's surface in some ways—to cut down on his drinking and modify his speech, perhaps. But if we go deeper than this we find little in his moral character that we would need—or care—to change.

So far our defense of Holden has been negative: we have attempted to explain away his apparent faults. But even if our arguments are not accepted, the positive qualities in Holden Caulfield are such that the reader is forced to admit that he is an admirable character—and note that "forced" is, for most people, the wrong word here; despite his supposed sins, Holden is immediately likable. Perhaps the greatest reason for our instinctive approval is that his goodness is not of the stern and uncompromising sort. He adheres to no rigid plan or order of righteousness. He presumes not to judge, though he is always evaluating. Replacing that formalized virtue which seems to be the best that most of us can achieve is the same force which we have seen vitiating his potential for ill: his overriding concern for others. In his relationship with his fellow man, Holden refuses rules when they interfere with this concern; he ignores custom when it is not applicable to a human situation. He replaces rules and regulations of propriety with his own gifts of intelligence, empathy, justice, and good taste. Indeed, he appears to have found a truth which is denied to most of us, though we live to be five times his age: he has learned to treat everyone he encounters as an individual human being; he never attempts to force people into preconceived pigeonholes or categories. Perhaps this is his greatest virtue.

Holden's concern for people as individuals is the basis of many of his best qualities. As we have seen, he is willing to admit the power that sex exerts, but is able to resist that power when it would reduce the dignity of the individual he is with. The "closest [he] ever got to necking" with Jane Gallagher was when she was crying and he attempted to comfort her. Despite the force of his developing sexual desire, his great delight with Jane is holding hands, which to his sensitive taste becomes almost an art, a fulfilling experience. "All you knew was, you were happy. You really were."

Holden's concern for others (it is time to give it its better name: love) is manifested in many other ways. Perhaps we can come close to Holden in terms of his love for Allie, Phoebe, and Jane, although the extent of his affection for his dead brother is probably beyond most of us (see pp. 49-50, 129). But it is Holden's love for *anybody*—for two nuns he meets in a restaurant (we remember that he is "sort of an atheist," and that Catholics usually disturb him), for dumpy out-of-town girls he meets in a night club, even for Ackley and Stradlater and Sunny and "old Maurice"—which makes him a superior individual. Throughout the novel Holden has made the usual human commitments: some people he has liked better than others; for some he has felt disgust and even contempt. But as he reaches the end of his story, even the sharpest of these distinctions disappears as Holden's love for humanity in its totality—though he manages to keep its individuality intact—encompasses all: "About all I know is, I sort of *miss* everybody I told about."

We have already suggested some causes of this kind of love in Holden, but perhaps the most important engendering *quality* is what might be called his potential for duality. In general, we prefer things to come in one's: a character is either good or bad, an idea acceptable or rejectable; a question has but one answer, and white is strictly white, and black can only be black. But Holden is able to accept the duality of things. He can both like and dislike something, as with sexual perversion, or old Sally Hayes, or Ernie, the good but corny piano player. He can appreciate the rudeness of Marsalla's action (p. 23), but also enjoy its humor. He hates the "phoniness" (a favorite word) of Lillian Simmons, but feels sorry for her just because he dislikes her. Holden is incapable of that judgment of others in terms of one part of their nature only, as when we befriend a country just because it opposes Communism, or vote for a presidential candidate because we like his face, his wife, or his war record. Holden must see each individual in his totality, and while there is usually something that requires condemnation, there is always something that demands sympathy. In large part it may be said that Holden's superiority to common humanity rests upon this ability to accept the duality of the nature of things.

We have attempted to supply a few clues to the virtuous nature of Holden Caulfield. But does he have limitations, as we have also suggested? Let us hope he has, for perfection is not known to man, and if Salinger has drawn his hero without a fault, we will soon realize that such a character has little to do with us, and will lose interest in him.

We have already done away with the common conception of sin as applied to Holden, and can probably agree that only the most puritanical will wish to damn him for such things as drinking, swearing, or lusting after women. But are there more serious weaknesses in Holden's nature? Is it possible, for example, that his very goodness may, from one point of view, be considered a fault? (When we reach such a problem, we have begun to discover the excellence of Salinger's creation, for a fictional character may be said to be great when he can be disagreed on, argued about, even as we discuss the figures of history. And in literature we have an advantage over history, where the figure recedes from us as time passes, so that it becomes more difficult to evaluate him. Holden is alive and immediate forever in the pages of his story, and we can all meet him and judge him through our personal acquaintance.)

We may investigate the problem of Holden's weakness by considering two things: society's effect upon him, and his effect upon society. As for the first, we can agree immediately that the effect is bad. Society is inimical. Against the boy's arrows of sincerity, honesty, and eager individuality, it throws up defenses of pretense, phoniness, and tight little cliques. When Holden attempts to think, he is met by clichés. When he searches for a formula to live by, he is swamped by dogma and narrow system. When he turns to those who are older and should provide guidance, they fail him. Indeed, the adults of this novel (and they, of course, *are* society—the world toward which Holden, as a boy of sixteen, is growing) are all either vicious or dull or weak. Though he meets several who are good to him, he finds no one who is of real help in his attempt to fit himself to the social order. His schoolmate's mother may be kind to him in a casual encounter on a train, but apparently she is incapable of doing much even for her own son, whom Holden describes as "doubtless the biggest bastard that ever went to Pency, in the whole crumby history of the school." When Holden looks for help he finds only the sickly Professor Spencer at Pency Prep and the probably homosexual Mr. Antolini, who gives him advice he is not yet ready to understand, and then upsets him by making advances. Perhaps his parents adore him, but when he feels the need for home it is to his young sister Phoebe that he turns, taking precautions not to be discovered by his mother, who would not understand. Holden gets very little help, and considerable hindrance, from the adult world.

Faced with such an environment, what is a young man to do? Three possible responses may be suggested: he can reject it; he can work to improve it; he can conform to it. We cheer Holden's determination not to surrender to the last of these three, as we too often do. But we fear that of the two choices left to him, Holden has taken the worse, and had rejected society. Most of the things he does (or refrains from doing) seem to point up this rejection. Why does Holden fail in school? Not because he is lazy or stupid, we may believe, for his intelligence and energy are demonstrable in many parts of the novel. But education is a part of maturing, and Holden does not want to grow up lest he become a part of the world of phoniness and weakness which he sees all around him. Holden likes the museum because things there don't change; he doesn't like it because it reminds him that all else *must* change: "Certain things they should stay the way they are." Everywhere we see Holden turning back to the world of childhood for his delight and security. Again, it is to Phoebe that he turns, not to his parents. He constantly speaks of the memories and activities of his childhood, of the pleasure which the company of children can bring. It is the innocent and playful part of *Hamlet* (where Laertes and Ophelia are "horsing around") that he likes best; he cannot appreciate the rest of the play, which is concerned with the terrible necessity of making adult decisions and performing adult actions. Holden rejects such a frightening world in favor of his brother Allie, who need never grow into that world because he is dead.

Rejection of the things of this world has not always been considered a weakness in man; why must we so consider it in Holden? The answer lies in the extent to which Holden fails as a human being because of this rejection. One does not live by merely existing, but by achieving and by becoming, and Holden seems determined not to become anything and not to do anything. In *The Catcher* he accomplishes nothing—doesn't in fact, even finish anything. And probably never will, for we see no change in him at the end of the story (perhaps the most damning fact in the novel is that Holden's telling of his story seems to have done nothing for him). In crucial situations we see him vacillate, evade, and withdraw. One of the most painful of these is his refusal to see Jane Gallagher in a situation near the beginning of the novel. He has just learned that she (to whom he seems to have come closer than any other human being, with the exception of his younger siblings) is on a date with his unscrupulous roommate, and he fears that Stradlater (which sounds like a tag-name) will dishonor her. But when Stradlater invites him to speak to Jane, he refuses—he is not in the mood. Only when Stradlater returns from the date, when it is too late to do anything for Jane (if indeed anything need be done), does he act, and then his action is of course useless. Later, in New York, he considers and then rejects the idea of calling Jane up. Jane poses a threat to Holden, for his relationship to her cannot continue to be immature; it must soon become that of man and woman. Instead, he calls up old Sally, whom he likes much less, but who will not force him to any adult action. With Sally, he concocts impossible and immature schemes of escape from his environment, reminiscent of Jack Burden's Western trip in *All the King's Men*. Later, he again dreams of a neverland to which he may escape from adulthood—this time with a dumb woman, who will make no demands on him for mature communication.

When Holden does make an attempt to enter the world of adult responsibility, he fails. He cannot have intercourse with girls because they tell him to stop, and he has to stop lest he hurt them. He cannot make love even to a prostitute—partly, as we have seen, because he feels sorry for her, but also because he is disturbed by the adult role he is attempting to play. When he thinks about what kind of a job he would like (pp. 223-4), he rejects them all, because he realizes that even in the best of them he might work some evil upon himself or upon the world. Instead, he wants an ideal but impossible job of catching children before they wander over a cliff. His misunderstanding of the song here is important: the real words of the tune are, "If a body meet a body, coming through the rye,/If a body greet a body, need a body cry?" It is a love song, investigating the nature of mature sexual relationships. But Holden has heard the song from the lips of a child who mistakenly sings, "If a body catch a body . . ." and for him it becomes the song of a savior; he will not meet and love and endure the chances of human intercourse, but will be a Christlike figure, incapable of hurting anyone, guaranteed to help all, to catch children before they fall into—what? Adulthood, perhaps—a state that is ugly enough as we see it in *The Catcher,* but a state we must grow toward or die.

Let us consider Holden's evaluation of adults in greater detail. He finds them pitiable ("depressing"), their lives even more harassed than those of children. Adults, he feels, are already formed, caught by the mechanization of routine. It is too late for you once you have grown up: ". . . there wouldn't be marvelous places to go after I went to college and all. . . . It'd be entirely different. We'd have to go downstairs in elevators with suitcases and stuff. We'd have to phone up everybody and tell 'em good-by and send 'em postcards from hotels and all. And I'd be working in some office, making a lot of dough, and riding to work in cabs and Madison Avenue buses, and reading newspapers, and playing bridge all the time, and going to the movies and seeing a lot of stupid shorts and coming attractions and newsreels." So, Holden reasons, if you don't grow up you won't be in this helpless, pitiful state. Kids are freer; they don't look ridiculous. "It's funny. You take adults, they look lousy when they're asleep and they have their mouths way open, but kids don't. Kids look all right. They can even have spit all over the pillow and they still look all right." To the adult, experience is regulated; new sensation (i.e., living) is gone. As William Wiegund says in his *Chicago Review* article, "[Holden] tries to guard each experience from falling into oblivion." Holden is right in his estimation of the immobilizing quality of adulthood. But in his rejection, in his attempt to escape from it, he has fallen into another kind of stasis: eternal childhood.

We may better understand the meaning and the result of Holden's failure if we compare him to two literary figures, one an individual, and one a type. The individual, who is similar to Holden, is Prince Myshkin of Dostoyevsky's *The Idiot*. The Prince is an innocent and saintly man, but this becomes his very defect: no one so good, so naive, Dostoyevsky seems to be saying, can act effectively in this world. One must partake of his environment—even of its imperfections—to be of use in it. Holden's almost complete desire to do only good may similarly prevent him from accomplishing anything.

Quite different from such a character is the tragic hero as he is commonly seen in Western literature. One great situation which the tragic hero constantly faces is the dilemma. He learns that it is impossible to act in this world without sinning, without causing evil. But he learns too that it is absolutely necessary for man to act, for if he does not—if he refuses to take the chance, will not attempt to become as well as to be, withdraws his hand from the work he sees before him to be done—then he is not a man. Tragedy is scrupulously and terribly honest. It does not pretend, like certain superficial and deceptive concepts of our time, that it is easy to be good if we will only try, that Utopia is achievable, that the rewards of such virtue as man can attain are not only virtue itself but also the good things of this life, including freedom from sin. Like the tragic hero, Holden is learning that to do is to sin. But unlike Hamlet or Macbeth or Oedipus, he cannot make his tragic commitment to action; he cannot accept sinfulness as a part of his nature. He looks at the adult world—phony, weak, self-deceiving, corrupt—and decides that he would rather not be than become a member of that world. We have said that Holden's great virtue is his acceptance of duality in others. Perhaps his great vice is his inability to accept it in himself.

At the end of his story a doctor asks him if, when he is well again, he will apply himself in school—if he will seek to finish something, to work at the growing-up process. Holden's answer shows that he has not changed: he thinks it is a stupid question, for how can you tell what you are going to do at any future moment? Children cannot tell, of course; in fact, not many adults can be certain. But a part of becoming an adult is the increasing ability to determine what one will at least attempt to do, and the ability to go on and do it. One week a child wants to be a fireman, the next week a policeman, and the next a movie star. But the young adult in college reduces his choices to a few, and finally commits himself to an occupation. Not so poor Holden: if he is going to become anything, he will do so only under ideal conditions which guarantee perfection, the total absence of wrongdoing. Otherwise he won't play.

Throughout the novel people ask Holden, "When in *hell* are

you going to grow up?" Resisting the temptation to make metaphysical play with the italicized word, we may simply answer, "Never." Though Holden is lovable and perhaps even saintly, he is not a hero in the tragic sense of accepting the terms of life. Life instead defeats Holden, and so his story is a sad, a pessimistic one. We usually think of tragedy as being sad, but in a way it is not: Hamlet may die, but his greatness gives us promise for the human race, and we feel better about things when we have met him. He has been defeated, but his defeat has been only external; no one has conquered the inner Hamlet. On the other hand, Holden may make us laugh and love him, but he must also make us sad because his defeat is internal: he seems willing to quit, and the picture he leaves with us is that of man unable to take action within his environment. Not only is there no hope for Holden, but there is no hope for any of us if young men like him do not acquire from somewhere—from religion, from humanism, from simple inner courage—the strength to fight to improve all of us, even if there is not much chance of their succeeding. Poor Holden is willing at last to abandon us to the Sally's and the Lillian's of this world; Goliath has conquered David, and the Philistines are upon us.

And yet if this is true—or if it is the whole truth—why is our final response to *The Catcher in the Rye* not one of discouragement, of despair? Though some readers undoubtedly do feel this way as they finish the novel, many more emerge from the experience with the feeling that something positive and assertive has been said, that something good and fruitful can be found in Holden's story. If this feeling is correct, we must look for some modification of our stern indictment of Holden Caulfield.

After all, we must remember that he is a boy of seventeen as he tells us his story. It is true that David was even younger, but the Goliath he faced was less formidable than the monster

Holden is up against. We may ask ourselves whose fault it is that this youth fails. Is Salinger calling attention to internal weaknesses in the nature of one boy, or is he exposing serious faults in society? Some readers will want to place most of the responsibility on Holden alone. It is true that society is not amenable to him, but is it not harmful to all of us? We learn to live in this society in order to attempt to improve it; Holden's inability to do this means that he is weak and, despite his innate goodness, inferior to the rest of us. Society should not be blamed for the ineffectuality of the individual.

But perhaps there is a better interpretation. It is true that Holden fails as hero, but is there not something more heroic, something nobler in his defeat than in many of our victories? Would we not prefer Holden vanquished to, say, Stradlater or Ernest Morrow or George-from-Andover triumphant? We are taught to love Holden in his defeat, and to hate the brute that has beaten him. It is only in these terms that the novel acquires significance: as a delineation of a boy's limitations, its meaning is narrow, but as a loving and tolerant and even amused but still stern indictment of our way of life, it reaches that plane of significance which justifies our deep interest in it.

Perhaps, after all, Holden's defeat is not meaningless or negative—how can it be? Literature is never defeatist, never meaningless; its very creation is an act of assertion. Holden's defeat teaches us the need for and the value of a victory—the need to work, imperfect as we are, toward a society in which Holden Caulfield could grow and flourish, toward an environment which would teach him the necessity of evil and phoniness and even despair, not through the words of a homosexual schoolteacher, but through the love of his parents and the actions of those he admires—through the very conduct of society itself.

The final judgment of Holden may be that he is both more and less than we are. It is true that he is defeated and ineffective, whereas we are able to function within our social structure and endeavor to improve it. But it is also true that Holden is the justification of our work, the youth for whom we try to make the world better, so that he can make it best. We cannot give Holden a perfect world—if we could, there would be no need for him. But we must find a way to give him an environment which will not destroy him before he has really begun to fight for us. For if there were no Holden Caulfield, we may believe, there would be no chance for—perhaps no need for—any of us.

Questions for Study and Discussion

CHAPTER I

1] What is the "David Copperfield kind of crap" to which Holden refers? Why doesn't he (or the author) "feel like going into it"? Do you accept the reasons Holden gives?

2] Is the story really about "madman stuff"? In what sense is it, or is it not?

3] Why does Holden exaggerate so much?

4] "I'm not going to tell you my whole goddam autobiography or anything," Holden tells us. But why does he bother to tell us any of his story?

5] Why did D. B.'s short story, "The Secret Goldfish," "kill" Holden? What kinds of things kill Holden or knock him out? What do these things tell you about him?

6] Holden says he hates movies; do you think he really does? Why does he continue to see them if he hates them? What are his reasons for hating them? (See what he has to say about movies elsewhere in the book.) How do the movies and Holden's feelings about them fit into the total pattern of the novel?

7] Why does Holden assume that the guy on the horse in the magazine ads for Pencey Prep is a "hot-shot"? What is there about Holden as we come to know him in the book that would lead him to such an assumption?

8] What are we to derive from the discussion of the football game?

9] Holden's description of Selma Thurmer is extremely unflattering; how does he feel about her as a person? Why does he feel this way? Is this feeling typical of Holden?

10] Holden finds humor in the fact that the fencing team ostracized him for losing the foils. Would you be amused if this happened to you? What do you learn about Holden from his reaction, and from the entire incident of the fencing team?

11] As Holden prepares to leave Pencey, he stands around trying to "feel some kind of good-by." What does he mean? What do you make of the memory that helps him to feel a good-by?

12] When Holden crosses the road to visit Mr. Spencer, he feels that he is "sort of disappearing." Can you recall and describe a similar feeling? Near the end of the novel Holden prays to his dead brother Allie not to let him disappear as he crosses streets in New York. Is there any connection?

13] How often does Holden qualify what he says by a modifying word, phrase, or clause? Why does he do this? Does his use of modifiers throw any light on the psychology of Holden? —on the theme of the novel?

14] What is Holden's attitude toward his reader? How can you tell?

CHAPTER II

1] Comment on the characterization of Mr. Spencer. What does Holden seem to think of him? (Note that he nods his head all the time, while Holden shakes his head all the time; is there any meaning in this?) Why does Salinger have Holden make this visit before he leaves Pencey? Does it prepare us for anything that happens later? Is it comparable to any other scenes?

2] "If you get on the side where all the hot-shots are, then [life is] a game, all right, I'll admit that. But if you get on the *other* side, where there aren't any hot-shots, then what's a game about it? Nothing. No game." What is Holden's definition of a "hot-shot"? Which side does he choose to be on?

QUESTIONS FOR STUDY AND DISCUSSION

How is his choice related to his own problem ("this madman stuff")?

3] Why do you think Salinger gives his sixteen-year-old protagonist gray hair? Start with the paragraph which mentions this and see what themes you can trace through the rest of the novel.

4] Why is "grand" a phony word for Holden? What people use this word in the novel? Find and discuss other words which Salinger uses for a similar purpose.

5] Holden tries to talk to Mr. Spencer, but reports that he "wasn't even listening. He hardly ever listened to you when you said something." Why is it important to Holden that Spencer doesn't listen to him? Does he feel the same way about other people in the story? Do they really fail to listen, or are his fears ungrounded? Can you make a case for incommunication as a pattern or theme in *The Catcher*?

6] Why does Holden consider it a dirty trick when Spencer reads his exam paper? What kind of moral judgment is being made?

7] In his exam paper, and later at the Museum of Natural History, Holden expresses his interest in Egyptian mummies. What does this interest tell us about Holden?

8] Near the end of this scene we learn that Spencer knows the answers to questions he has earlier asked of Holden; what is the meaning of this?

9] This chapter begins a series of references to the ducks from the lagoon in Central Park. What do you make of Holden's interest in the ducks? Holden is talking to Mr. Spencer when he begins to think of the ducks; what is he talking about?

10] Mr. Spencer asks Holden how he feels about his expulsion from Pencey; later, others ask him similar questions (notably Mr. Antolini and, at the end, D. B.). Note the circumstances under which these questions are asked, the kind of people who ask them, and the responses of Holden.

11] Comment on Holden's reason for leaving Elkton Hills. To what other incidents in the novel can you relate this one? Does a pattern of any kind form?

12] In what sense are Holden and Spencer "on opposite sides of the pole"?

13] Compare Holden's departures from the homes of Mr. Spencer and Mr. Antolini.

14] Holden says he would never yell "Good Luck!" at anybody and comments, "It sounds terrible when you think about it." Why does it sound terrible to him?

CHAPTER III

1] What is wrong with Mr. Ossenburger? Do other characters in *The Catcher* share his faults in increasing or decreasing gradations of seriousness? Comment upon Salinger's technique of giving us brief glimpses of people who never appear again in the story; what are the aims of this technique?

2] References to Holden's red hunting hat begin in this chapter, and continue throughout the novel. To what uses does Salinger put the hat? Does it acquire the status of a symbol?

3] Explore and explain Holden's comments on literature in this chapter.

4] Discuss Ackley in terms of question 1 (above).

5] Compare and contrast Ackley and Stradlater, and discuss Holden's attitude toward each. (Material in Chapter IV will be of use to you here, too.)

CHAPTER IV

1] What point is Holden making when he talks about the attitudes of Stradlater and Ackley toward themes and basketball?

2] Consider the relationship between Holden and Ackley in

QUESTIONS FOR STUDY AND DISCUSSION

Chapter III, and that of Holden and Stradlater in Chapter IV. How do these relationships differ? Are they at all similar? Is there any kind of continuity or progression between them?

3] In this chapter Salinger introduces the name of Jane Gallagher and gives us a bit of her background, but makes us wait for the rest of her story until Chapter XI—why? Does he commonly split material up in this way? What is gained and lost by doing so? What do you think should be said about the organization of the novel?

4] Why doesn't Holden go down to see Jane? To what other incidents in the novel can you relate this?

5] Why is Holden fascinated by the fact that Jane likes to keep her kings in the back row when she plays checkers?

CHAPTER V

1] Use the paragraph in which Holden makes a snowball to illustrate Salinger's method of presenting character.

2] Holden's younger brother Allie is introduced in this chapter. What is his function in the novel? Collect all references to him, and write as complete a character study as you can. What do we learn about Holden from his comments on Allie? In what ways can Allie be contrasted with D. B.? In what ways is he similar to Phoebe?

3] Allie had red hair and Holden has a red hat, which he wears backwards. Any comment? Do people who try to find meaning in such things push too hard? How does one decide?

4] A casual reading of *The Catcher* leaves the impression that the novel is disorganized and even fragmentary. What evidences of solid planning do you find in it? For example, has time been plotted carefully? Start with references to time in this chapter, and go on to other places where time is mentioned.

5] If you discussed the question of Holden's habit of exaggeration (Chapter I), you doubtless gave considerable attention to his diction. Holden seems to throw words around rather loosely—consider his use of "madman," "crazy," and "goddam," for example. Can you discover some precision in his application of such words? Holden calls Ackley "crazy" at the end of this chapter; is this meaningless? Is it exaggeration? In what sense has Holden himself been described as crazy in this chapter?

6] Does Holden's concern with the troubles and shortcomings of people form a pattern of sympathy? Why is he so sensitive to people's faults and flaws?

CHAPTER VI

1] Holden starts this chapter with a short lecture on himself as worrier. Does the novel prove him right? Write as complete a statement of what worries Holden as you can make.

2] Consider the stress on Stradlater's dating exploits and Holden's concern about his dating Jane; is it possible that the name "Ward Stradlater" has symbolic meaning? How about other names—Ackley; Holden Caulfield; Phoebe; D. B.; Allie?

3] Contrast Stradlater's sexual habits with Holden's. Which, if either, seems more normal for a teenage boy? Which, judged from several points of view, is better?

4] This chapter is climaxed by the fight between Holden and Stradlater. What are the implications of this fight? Whose fault is it? What does it tell you about Holden? How would you have acted if you had been Holden?—if you had been Stradlater?

5] Is there anything thematically significant in Holden's not being able to make a fist after his demonstration following Allie's death? "I'm not too tough," Holden says, and adds, "I'm a pacifist, if you want to know the truth." How would Holden define the word "pacifist"?

6] At the ends of Chapters IV, V, and VI Holden suddenly

comes back to the subject of Ackley. Why does Holden think of Ackley so much?

CHAPTER VII

1] Does this chapter strengthen or weaken your ideas about the comparison or contrast between Ackley and Stradlater which you began in Chapter III? Holden has just had a fight with Stradlater; what is the nature of his relationship with Ackley here? Holden leaves Stradlater shouting insults at him, and leaves Ackley shaking hands ironically. What significances are there in these conclusions of relationships?

2] Holden speaks of people of all ages as "old": old Spencer, old Stradlater, old Ackley, old Ernie, old Mrs. Morrow, old Maurice, old Jane, old Phoebe, et cetera. Why does he do this? What does the word "old" seem to mean to him? What does the whole concept of age mean to him? (You may need to re-read the whole story carefully to find enough material for a satisfactory answer to this question. Keep a sharp eye for things like the following: 1) in Chapter IV he attacks Stradlater just after his roommate has said, on giving up Miss Fitzgerald, that she is "too old for you."; 2) Holden's gray hair makes him look older than he is—at least so he thinks; he still has trouble ordering drinks in a bar; 3) the ugliness of age disturbs Holden—witness his reaction to Mr. Spencer in his bathrobe, and "Old guys' legs, at beaches and places . . ."— Chapter II.)

3] What reasons are there for Holden's refusal to tell Ackley what the fight was about?

4] Compare Holden's actions in Ackley's room to Ackley's actions in Holden's room.

5] In a dormitory full of boys his age, Holden is "sad and lonesome." Why? Locate other passages in which he suddenly becomes lonely, and determine whether certain kinds of things or situations make him that way.

6] What do you learn about Holden from his preparations for his trip to New York?

7] Chapter VII ends the Pencey Prep section of *The Catcher*; Chapter VIII finds him on his way to New York, where the "main" events of the novel take place. Why has Salinger taken so long (about one fourth of the novel) to get his hero away from the school? What are his purposes in these seven chapters?

CHAPTER VIII

1] What is the function of Mrs. Morrow? Why do you think Holden likes her? How does he treat her? How does she treat him? In what way does this conversation on the train prepare us for the events that will occur in New York?

2] Holden's invitation to Mrs. Morrow to join him in a cocktail begins a long series of incidents in which he drinks or tries to drink. Decide what we are to learn about Holden from these incidents.

3] Evaluate Holden's self-accusation that he is a liar.

CHAPTER IX

1] Holden calls Phoebe "roller-skating skinny." What does that mean?—what have roller skates to do with being skinny? Are such expressions the reflection of a complicated association of past experience? Do they differ from mere connotation? What is the relationship of such expression to Holden's problems?

2] Why does Holden place Stradlater among the perverts of the hotel? Hasn't his objection to Stradlater been that he is only too well adjusted sexually?

3] Phoebe "writes books all the time. Only, she doesn't finish them," Holden tells us. Holden doesn't finish his book, either. What is the author's point in this non-finishing of stories? What has it to do with the psychology, philosophy, and mentality of Holden and Phoebe? What has it to do with Holden's problem? In his no-end short story, "Seymour—An Introduction," Salinger has Buddy Glass react against stories with endings. (Indeed, Buddy is against "Beginnings and Middles" too!) And yet we are told that all stories must have a beginning, middle, and end. What do you make of all this?

4] Analyze Holden's comments on sex in this chapter.

5] What is depressing about the prospect of the three girls getting up early to see the first show at Radio City Music Hall?

6] In Chapter IV Holden learned that Jane Gallagher was at Pencey, but he did not try to see her. Now he thinks about calling her, but decides not to. What are his reasons? Why do you think he rejects the idea of contacting someone he obviously likes so much?

7] Why does Holden call Faith Cavendish instead of Jane? Compare the two girls. Why does Holden fail to make a date "for cocktails or something"?

CHAPTER X

1] Holden interrupts his account of going to the Lavender Room to talk of his sister Phoebe. Does something remind him of her? Why does he speak of her here?

2] Which qualities of Phoebe does Holden find most important? Are these qualities similar to those of other people he likes—those of Jane, for instance?

3] On the other hand, Holden is not fond of the blonde he dances with in the night club—in fact, he classifies her as a moron. What other people are also called morons by Holden? What qualities seem to make one a candidate for this name?

CHAPTER XI

1] Chapter XI is given over entirely to memory, as Holden

sits in the hotel lobby. What is the purpose of this digressive interlude?

2] Characterize Jane and her relationship with Holden. In what ways is she similar to him?

3] What does Holden mean by the expression, "That killed me"?

4] Why does Jane's tear dropping on the checkerboard bother Holden?

5] Go back to the end of Chapter VII and review Holden's plans for his stay in New York. Is he following them so far? What is he doing?

6] What is Holden's attitude toward music, as expressed here and elsewhere in the novel? What is significant about what he likes and doesn't like? Is his taste in music similar to his taste in literature, the movies, and the theater?

CHAPTER XII

1] Holden's experience with the first cabbie apparently hasn't discouraged him, for now he asks a second taxi driver about the ducks in Central Park. How does Horwitz's response compare with that of the first driver? How does Holden feel about him?

2] Analyze Holden's responses to Ernie; how do they fit into his general responses to life? He blames "people" for ruining Ernie, and condemns "people" again at the end of the chapter. Is he then a misanthropist? How does he feel about the individuals who make up "people" as he looks them over?

3] Of what significance is Lillian Simmons? Why doesn't Holden like her? Is she one of the "people" who have ruined Ernie?

4] "If you want to stay alive, you have to say that stuff ['Glad to have met you'] though," says Holden at the end of this chapter. What does he mean by "alive"? Is he just exaggerating again?

QUESTIONS FOR STUDY AND DISCUSSION 29

CHAPTER XIII

1] Examine the case Holden makes for his own cowardice. What evidence do you find elsewhere in the novel to help you accept or reject his self-accusation?

2] Consider the significance of Holden's meeting with Sunny, the prostitute. Look for earlier remarks about sex which may help you to understand this incident more completely. Compare Holden's attitude toward Sunny with his feelings about Jane and Sally. Describe his actions as the scene begins and progresses; what do they seem to imply?

CHAPTER XIV

1] This is the first of two situations in which Holden talks to his dead brother Allie. Compare the two; are they alike or different? What can you conclude about Holden from them?

2] In this chapter also is one of several references to religion to be found throughout *The Catcher*. What do you make of these references? What is the attitude toward religion, on the whole? Does the passage in this chapter seem profane to you? Why, or why not?

3] Holden is generous—even careless—with his money. He gives ten dollars to the nuns he meets briefly; he pays the night club bill for the girls who treat him rudely. But in the previous chapter (XIII) he refuses to pay five more dollars to Sunny, even though he is eager to get rid of her. And in this chapter he resists the threats of Maurice, even though he has called himself a coward. Why does Holden make such a fuss over five dollars?

4] Holden's narration of his childish pretense after Maurice had punched him ("I sort of started pretending I had a bullet in my guts. Old Maurice had plugged me.") is followed by, "The goddam movies. They can ruin you." What is the connection between the movies and the pretense? Holden has insisted all along that he hates the movies, and his taste runs to good films. Why, then, does he act out this silly scene from a Grade-C cinema? And why, in this moment of real pain, does he act out an imaginary role (or better, recreate a movie role)? In what sense can the movies "ruin you"?

5] What (if we can believe him at this point) brings Holden near to a suicide attempt at the end of this chapter? What keeps him from jumping out the window?

CHAPTER XV

1] Why do you think Holden is in the mood to call Sally Hayes instead of Jane? What is his attitude toward each girl? Comment on his attitude toward Sally in the light of his remarks on girls in Chapter IX.

2] For the first time in the novel, Holden speaks of his father at some length. What do you make of this and other references to his parents? Do you trust his picture of them? Why?

3] Why is so much made of suitcases in this chapter? Does Salinger make them representative of something in people? Does he do this with other things in the novel—that is, use things to represent some aspect of human nature?

4] Holden calls women of the Salvation Army "babes." Many readers will dislike this, feeling that he is being youthfully rude. How do you feel about the expression? What does such word choice tell you about Holden as a speaker? Illustrate your answer with other words and phrases that he uses.

5] Evaluate Holden's comments about the nuns; what would you say his idea of a nun is? What do you make of his conversation with them?

6] What is the point of Holden's feelings about Catholics? What is the similarity to the suitcases that he mentions? What is it that Holden is against?

CHAPTER XVI

1] Why does Holden believe the record "Little Shirley Beans"

QUESTIONS FOR STUDY AND DISCUSSION 31

will "knock old Phoebe out"? Explain this sentence about the record: "If a white girl was singing it, she'd make it sound *cute* as hell, but old Estelle Fletcher knew what she was doing, and it was one of the best records I ever heard."

2] Here occurs the passage that gives the novel its title. What can you make of this passage by itself? Now, add to it later comments on the same idea, and see what you can conclude.

3] What do Holden's comments on acting add to your understanding of him?

4] What is it about the museum that attracts Holden?

5] What is the connection between the little girl in the park, the skate key, Phoebe, and Holden?

CHAPTER XVII

1] State as precisely as possible the contribution to Holden's character made in the opening paragraph of this chapter.

2] In this chapter Holden makes an important attack upon his society, and offers a plan for escaping it. Explain his attack carefully, and comment on his method of escape. What are your conclusions about Holden Caulfield?

3] When Holden says, "A horse is at least *human*, for God's sake," what does he really mean? What does he regard as being "human"? How are all things he enumerates to Sally related to his problem?

4] When Holden admits, "I'm in bad shape," how much of his problem and his condition does he realize? Would you agree with him that he doesn't "get hardly anything out of anything"? What does he mean by this outcry? And why has he uttered it to Sally, who is certainly no Allie, D. B., Phoebe, or Jane?

5] Holden says Sally does not see what he means at all. Do you? Does Holden himself see what he means? How is it all tied in with Holden's conversation and experience with Sally?

Do these bring him to the extremity of his elopement proposal? To what extent do all of his experiences add up to the moment of proposal?

6] In several places in the novel Holden comments on what he thinks of himself and how he would react to meeting someone just like himself. What does Holden think of Holden? Does he like people who are somewhat like himself? Does he understand people who are like him?

CHAPTER XVIII

1] Why does Holden think Jesus would like the kettle drummer at Radio City Music Hall? Could you have predicted this from what you know of Holden?

2] Speaking about the picture he sees at the Music Hall, Holden says, "It was so putrid I couldn't take my eyes off it." What is that supposed to mean? The movie has been identified as *Random Harvest*; if you know it, evaluate Holden's comments upon it.

3] Why does Holden believe being drafted into the army would be one of the worst things that could happen to him?

4] The Caulfields are different from one another, and yet they seem to have great love and respect for each other. What knits them together so strongly? (If you have read Salinger's stories of the Glass family, you might compare the two families.)

CHAPTER XIX

1] Back in another bar, Holden starts talking about hating everybody again. What makes him say this? Compare the incident to the former scene in which Holden sits in a night club and speaks of hating people.

2] Luce is a little older than Holden and his age group; is he similar, in any way, to this group? Who in Holden's age group would you pick to grow up to be Luce? What is Salinger trying to say through this individual?

3] Evaluate Holden's conduct before Luce. Is he being himself? Is he acting? Why is he so curious about Luce?

4] Luce says, "I refuse to answer any typical Caulfield questions tonight." What is a "typical Caulfield question"? Does Luce answer any of them on this evening?

5] What evidence is there in other parts of the novel that Holden regards sex as a physical and spiritual experience?

6] Using this chapter as an example, consider the manner in which Salinger brings his chapter to a conclusion. Is he climactic? Anticlimactic? Does he underscore something by his conclusions?

CHAPTER XX

1] How different is the Wicker Bar from the way Holden sees it? The point of view employed by Salinger in this novel is more complex than casual consideration makes it seem. Analyze the point of view carefully and explain Salinger's reason for its complexities.

2] What kind of a drunk is Holden?

3] Holden uses telephones a great deal, and talks about them even more. What do telephones represent in the novel? What success does Holden find as a result of dialing or planning to dial?

4] What evidence is there in this chapter that Holden has not really accepted the fact that Allie is dead? What evidence is there that he has? How is his own future death linked in his mind with Allie's death? By what series of thoughts has Holden come to think of Allie, and then of Phoebe? To what extent is the whole novel an explanation of connections between Allie, Holden, and Phoebe?

CHAPTER XXI

1] Do you think Phoebe is a probable character? Is her relationship with her brother probable? What principles or standards help you to decide?

2] When Phoebe says that she put ink on a classmate's windbreaker, Holden asks, "What are you—a child, for God's sake?" This is one of the few times in the novel when Holden slurs childhood; critics generally see him as preferring it to adulthood. Are we to find any significance in Holden's statement here?

3] Compare this scene with the next one in which Holden and Phoebe meet. Are there significant parallels or contrasts?

CHAPTER XXII

1] Add the indictment of Pencey Prep here to the comments on it in the early chapters; what does it add up to? Are you on Holden's side?

2] "But you don't have to be a bad guy to depress somebody —you can be a *good* guy and do it," Holden tells Phoebe. Holden is often depressed by people. What is it about them that depresses him? Exactly what does he mean by "depress"?

3] What do you make of Holden's comments on the various professions? What do you think of his choice?

4] Can Holden be a catcher in the rye? Why? Some critics say that he is a catcher, for he keeps Phoebe from running away. Do you agree?

CHAPTER XXIII

1] Phoebe has said her prayers in the bathroom. Many scenes in this novel take place in bathrooms, or we hear about scenes in bathrooms. (A considerable portion of "Zooie," a later story, also is located in a bathroom.) Is there any significance in this?

2] What similarities are there between Mrs. Caulfield and her children?

QUESTIONS FOR STUDY AND DISCUSSION 35

3] Why does Holden begin to cry when Phoebe gives him her Christmas money? Why does he give her his hunting hat?

4] Holden constantly trips over things, as at the end of this chapter. Is there any significance in this?

CHAPTER XXIV

1] Are you surprised that Holden flunked the Oral Expression course?

2] Mr. Antolini says that Holden is riding for a fall. Where else in the novel do you encounter the idea of falling? Put all references together; what does it add up to?

3] What do you think of Mr. Antolini's evaluation of Holden's problem? Is he right? Is he helpful to Holden? Do you think he would make a good catcher? What do you make of the remainder of the chapter?

4] Is Mr. Antolini homosexual? Is it important to determine whether he is or not?

CHAPTER XXV

1] What is the meaning of Holden's fear that he will fall and disappear when he steps off the curb of each street? With what do you connect this?

2] Why does the obscenity scrawled on the school wall drive Holden "damn near crazy"? Can they be seen as the culmination of much of his fear during the story? Are they connected with Ackley, Jane, Phoebe, and children in general? Are they connected to Holden in his role as catcher in the rye? Why does he assume that "some perverty bum" and not a school child has written the message? Look back to other places where Holden uses the term "perverty"; what does it mean to him? To whom has he applied it? Have such people attempted to take advantage of Holden or of others? How is the message written on the wall related to perverts? What does the message symbolize for Holden?

3] Holden visits the mummies in this chapter, and here many of the recurrent items of the book are linked with them: children, perversion, bathrooms, and Holden's illness. What does this assembly mean?

4] Why does Holden begin to hate his sister when she pleads to run away with him? Does this fit the picture you have of him so far?

CHAPTER XXVI

1] Explain the last two sentences of the book.

2] It has been said that in form this novel is circular. What do you suppose this means? Do you agree that the novel is circular? If so, what has the form to do with the theme?

General Questions

1] Contrast Holden's private and public manners—his thoughts and his actions. One critic has said that the difference between what Holden thinks and what he says or does is the central problem of the novel. Decide what this statement means, and what you think of it.

2] Some readers of *The Catcher in the Rye* do not like Holden Caulfield, but probably almost everyone will agree that the author *wants* us to like his protagonist. How does he go about making us like him? How does his method differ from those of others who present teenagers—in novels for young people, or in motion picture scripts and television scenarios? How do you explain the inclusion of several things which would ordinarily make us dislike a boy—the profanity and vulgarity, the bad grammar, the apparent sacrilege, the disrespect for elders, the unconventional attitudes?

3] Many critics have commented on the tendency in the last hundred years or so to present youths as protagonists in novels. An extended investigation of this tendency should doubtless be reserved for the Ph.D. dissertation, but you may be interested in taking a small bite from one of the more interesting portions of the problem by comparing some aspect of *The Catcher* and another novel which has a young hero. For a start, we suggest *Huckleberry Finn* (Mark Twain), *The Red Badge of Courage* (Stephen Crane), *A Portrait of the Artist as a Young Man* (James Joyce), *An American Tragedy* (Dreiser), *Studs Lonigan* (Farrell), *Seventeen* (Tarkington), or *The Bear* (Faulkner). Begin by comparing the protagonists of the two novels you choose, then enlarge your consideration to such problems as the technique of presentation, the author's attitude toward his character, the use of point of view, the employment of humor, and the pervasive attitudes or philosophies. Then narrow your study down to one of these, and make as full an investigation of it as time and talent will allow.

4] The selection of a point of view is important to a novelist, for it strictly limits the way in which he may tell his story. Salinger chooses to let a seventeen-year-old boy narrate his novel. Do you think this was a good choice? What does he gain by allowing Holden to speak for himself? What would Salinger have gained if he had told the story in his own person, or had selected another character in the novel—say, D. B. or Phoebe or Mr. Antolini—to tell it?

5] In general, a good novel must have probability—we must be able to believe in its characters and actions. And yet we know from the beginning, don't we, that a novel is fiction and therefore untrue? What can a novelist do to convince us that his characters and their lives are real? (Enlist the aid of your instructor here.) To what extent is Salinger successful at this?

6] Another important requirement for fiction is conflict: we are rarely attracted to a story which does not pit people or forces against each other. Your discussion of some of the chapter questions has probably helped you to decide what conflicts exist in *The Catcher in the Rye*; now determine what the main or central conflict is, and state its nature as fully and precisely as you can. Consider such things as when you first became aware of the nature of the conflict, how the author intensifies it, and what its climax and resolution (if any) are.

7] Several of the chapter questions brought your attention

to the problem of the structure of *The Catcher in the Rye*. What have you decided about its structure? Is the novel held together by a plot—a chain-like sequence of events which lead to a climax and conclusion? Is the story loosely constructed —could we take an incident out of its present place and insert it somewhere else in the story without hurting either the incident or the novel as a whole? If you decide that the plot is not too important in *The Catcher*, try to find other devices which help the novel to achieve continuity and unity.

8] Several chapter questions directed your attention to symbols in *The Catcher*—Holden's hunting hat, the carrousel, suitcases, and so on. Now consider the novel's use of symbolism in its entirety. What kind(s) of symbols does Salinger use? Does he fit them into a system—do they relate to each other in some sort of pattern? What function(s) do the symbols perform?

9] Prepare for yourself a careful definition of the word "atmosphere" as it is applied to the novel. What is the atmosphere of *The Catcher in the Rye*? How does Salinger create this atmosphere?

10] Mark Twain's *Huckleberry Finn*, to which *The Catcher in the Rye* is often compared, has been called a "subversive" novel by several critics. Can Salinger's novel also be called subversive? From what point of view might it be so considered? If it is in any way subversive, should it therefore be condemned?

11] After submitting the manuscript of *The Catcher in the Rye* to a publisher (not the firm which did publish the book), Salinger withdrew his novel because, as he reportedly put it, "Why, the man thought Holden is crazy." What light (or perhaps darkness) does this incident throw on your reading of *The Catcher*?

Critical Comments

Explore more fully the following comments on *The Catcher in the Rye* which have been made by critics of this novel. (Consult the bibliography for full information on the articles from which these comments have been taken.)

From Leslie Fiedler, "Up from Adolescence."

"[The] theme which lies at the center of *Catcher in the Rye* [is] madness as the chief temptation of modern life, especially for the intelligent young. . . ."

From Maxwell Geismar, "The Wise Child and the *New Yorker* School of Fiction."

"Compact, taut and colorful, the first half of the novel presents in brief compass all the petty horrors, the banalities, the final mediocrity of the typical prep school. Very fine—and not sustained or fulfilled, as fiction. For the later sections of the narrative are simply an episodic account of Holden Caulfield's 'lost weekend' in New York City which manages to sustain our interest but hardly deepens our understanding."

From Frederick L. Gwynn and Joseph L. Blotner, *The Fiction of J. D. Salinger.*

"[Holden] sacrifices himself in a constant war against evil, even though he has a poignantly Manichean awareness of its ubiquity . . . his reward is to understand that if one considers humanity, one must love it. The text for Holden's behavior is his insistence . . . on absolutely primitive Christianity: 'Jesus never sent old Judas to hell!' "

From Ihab Hassan, "The Rare Quixotic Gesture."

"The retreat to childhood is not simply an escape; it is also a criticism, an affirmation of values which, for better or worse, we still cherish. . . ." "[Holden's] ultimate defense . . . is defenselessness."

"[Holden's response] to the dull or angry world about [him] is not simply one of withdrawal: it often takes the form of a strange, quixotic gesture. The gesture, one feels sure, is the bright metaphor of Salinger's sensibility, the center from which meaning drives, and ultimately the reach of his commitment to past innocence and current guilt. It is a gesture at once of pure expression and of expectation, of protest and prayer, of aesthetic form and spiritual content—as Blackmur would say, it is behavior that singes. There is often something prodigal and spontaneous about it, something humorous or whimsical, something that disrupts our habits of gray acquiescence and revives our faith in the willingness of the human spirit. But above all, it gives of itself as only a *religious* gesture can."

"As a 'neo-picaresque,' [*The Catcher in the Rye*] shows itself to be concerned far less with the education or initiation of an adolescent than with a dramatic exposure of the manner in which ideals are denied access to our lives and of the modes which mendacity assumes in our urban culture."

From Granville Hicks, "J. D. Salinger: The Search for Wisdom."

"Holden Caulfield is torn, and nearly destroyed, by the conflict between integrity and love. He is driven by the need not to be less than himself, not to accept what he knows to be base. On the other hand, he is capable of understanding and loving the persons to whom his integrity places him in opposition. The problem of values with which Salinger so persuasively confronts his sixteen-year-old is not exclusively a problem of adolescence."

From Seymour Krim, "Surface and Substance in a Major Talent."

"Salinger brings back to us the things we have taken for granted and that is why he evokes something close to love in his readers."

From David Leitch, "The Salinger Myth."

The reader learns about Holden not from what he does, nor even what he thinks, but from the way that he expresses his thoughts."

From Barry A. Marks, "Holden in the Rye."

"[*The Catcher in the Rye*] dramatizes, finally, ultimate issues rather than ultimate judgments. . . ."

From Dexter Martin, "Holden in the Rye."

"Like everybody else in the book Antolini fails to see that what ails Holden is the death of his brother, Allie ('All'), plus parental neglect. That is why the world seems full of phoniness to Holden."

From Arthur Mizener, "The Love Song of J. D. Salinger."

". . . a great deal of his most brilliant wit . . . is close to desperation."

"His immediate appeal is that he speaks our language, or, to be exact, makes a kind of poetry out of the raw materials of our speech."

"His people are wholly present, in devastating dramatic immediacy, in everything they say."

From Donald H. Reiman, "Holden in the Rye."

"Even though Holden is unable to evaluate fully his own experience, he has obviously chosen as his model of human life his sister Phoebe—still living, learning, reaching, loving—rather than his dead brother Allie, doomed to eternal childhood."

From Peter J. Seng, "The Fallen Idol: The Immature World of Holden Caulfield."

"[The story proper of *The Catcher in the Rye*] reads like an edited psychoanalysis, an illusion which is sustained by the rambling first person narrative."

"While Holden is quick to pass severe judgments on others he is not so quick to see the faults in himself."

From David L. Stevenson, "J. D. Salinger: The Mirror of Crisis."

"Whenever a character approaches hopelessness in a Salinger sketch, he is getting there by the route of the comic."

From Dan Wakefield, "The Search for Love."

"The things that Holden finds so deeply repulsive are things he calls 'phony'—and the 'phoniness' in every instance is the absence of love, and, often, the substitution of pretense for love. . . . Holden is repulsed because material values draw on what little store of love there is in the world and expend it on 'things' instead of people."

From William Wiegand, "J. D. Salinger: Seventy-Eight Bananas."

"Salinger has, in a measure, revived the dormant art of dialect in American fiction. His ear has detected innumerable idiomatic expressions that were simply unrecorded before."

"[Holden] is a victim not so much of society as of his own spiritual illness."

"Holden Caulfield's trouble . . . is not that he hates, or that he fears, or . . . that he has no goals—but rather that he has no capacity to purge his sensations. He is blown up like a balloon, or like a bananafish, with his memories."

A Salinger Bibliography

SALINGER'S FICTION (*Chronological*)

1940 "The Young Folks," *Story*, XVI (March-April), 26-30.
1941 "The Hang of It," *Collier's*, CVIII (July 12), 22.

"The Heart of a Broken Story," *Esquire*, XVI (September), 32, 131-133.

1942 "Personal Notes on an Infantryman," *Collier's*, CX (July 12), 96.

"The Long Debut of Lois Taggett," *Story*, XXI (September-October), 28-34.

1943 "The Varioni Brothers," *Saturday Evening Post*, CCXVI (July 17), 12-13, 76-77.

1944 "Both Parties Concerned," *Saturday Evening Post*, CCXVI (February 26), 14, 47-48.

"Soft-Boiled Sergeant," *Saturday Evening Post*, CCXVI (April 15), 18, 82, 84-85.

"Last Day of the Last Furlough," *Saturday Evening Post*, CCXVII (July 15), 26-27, 61-62, 64.

"Once a Week Won't Kill You," *Story*, XXV (November-December), 23-27.

1945 "A Boy in France," *Saturday Evening Post*, CCXVII (March 31), 21, 92.

"Elaine," *Story*, XXV (March-April), 38-47.

"This Sandwich Has No Mayonnaise," *Esquire*, XXIV (October), 54-56, 147-149.

"The Stranger," *Collier's*, CXVI (December 1), 18, 77.

"I'm Crazy," *Collier's*, CXVI (December 22), 36, 48, 51.

1946 "Slight Rebellion off Madison," *New Yorker*, XXII (December 21), 82-86.

1947 "A Young Girl in 1941 With No Waist at All," *Mademoiselle* (May), 222-223, 292-302.

"The Inverted Forest," *Cosmopolitan*, CXIII (December), 73-80, 85-86, 88, 90, 92, 95-96, 98, 100, 102, 104.

1948 "A Perfect Day for Bananafish," *New Yorker*, XXIII (January 31), 21-25. Reprinted in *Nine Stories* (q.v.).

"A Girl I Knew," *Good Housekeeping*, CXXVI (February), 36, 186, 188, 191-196.

"Uncle Wiggily in Connecticut," *New Yorker*, XXIV (March 20), 30-36. Reprinted in *Nine Stories* (q.v.).

"Just Before the War with the Eskimos," *New Yorker*, XXIV (June 5), 37-40. Reprinted in *Nine Stories* (q.v.).

"Blue Melody," *Cosmopolitan*, CXXV (September), 51-52, 112-119.

1949 "The Laughing Man," *New Yorker*, XXV (March 19), 27-32. Reprinted in *Nine Stories* (q.v.).

"Down at the Dinghy," *Harper's*, CXCVIII (April), 87-91. Reprinted in *Nine Stories* (q.v.).

1950 "For Esmé—with Love and Squalor," *New Yorker*, XXVI (April 8), 28-36. Reprinted in *Nine Stories* (q.v.).

1951 *The Catcher in the Rye*. New York: Little, Brown & Company, July.

"Pretty Mouth and Green My Eyes," *New Yorker*, XXVII (July 14), 20-24. Reprinted in *Nine Stories* (q.v.).

1953 "Teddy," *New Yorker*, XXVIII (January 31), 26-34. Reprinted in *Nine Stories* (q.v.).

"De Daumier-Smith's Blue Period," in *Nine Stories*. New York: Little, Brown & Co., April. Reprinted by the New American Library, 1954.

1955 "Franny," *New Yorker*, XXX (January 29), 24-32.

"Raise High the Roof Beam, Carpenters," *New Yorker*, XXXI (November 19), 51-58, 60, 62, 65-66, 68, 70, 72-74, 76, 78-80, 83-84, 86-92, 95-98, 100-105, 107-110.

1957 "Zooey," *New Yorker*, XXXIII (May 4), 32-42, 44, 47-48, 52, 54, 57-59, 62, 64, 67-68, 70, 73-74, 76-78, 83-84, 86-88, 91-94, 97-98, 100-104, 107-114, 117-135.

1959 "Seymour—An Introduction," *New Yorker*, XXXV (June 6), 42-52, 54, 57, 60, 62, 64, 66-67, 68, 71-72, 74, 76-78, 80, 82, 84, 89-90, 92-102, 105-116, 119.

1961 *Franny and Zooey*. Little, Brown & Company.

1963 *Raise High the Roof Beam, Carpenters*. Little, Brown & Company.

CRITICISM OF SALINGER'S FICTION (*Alphabetical*)

(NOTE: For early reviews of *The Catcher in the Rye*, see the following—*Christian Science Monitor* (July 19, 1951), 7; *Newsweek*, XXXVIII, 3 (July 16, 1951), 89-90; *New York Herald Tribune Sunday Book Review* (July 15, 1951), 3; *New York Herald Tribune* (July 16, 1951), 13; *New York Times Book Review* (July 15, 1951), 1; *New York Times* (July 16, 1951), 19; *Time*, LVIII, 3 (July 16, 1951), 96-97. A biographical sketch of Salinger entitled "On an Author," by J. K. Hutchens, appeared in the *New York Herald Tribune Sunday Book Review* (August 19, 1951), 2.)

Barr, Donald. "Saints, Pilgrims and Artists," *Commonweal*, LXVII (October 25, 1957), 88-90.

Branch, Edgar. "Mark Twain and J. D. Salinger: A Study in Literary Continuity," *American Quarterly*, IX, No. 2, Part 1 (Summer 1957), 144-158.

Browne, Robert M. "In Defense of Esme," *College English*, XXII, 8 (May 1961), 584-585.

Bryden, Ronald. "Living Dolls," *Spectator*, No. 6948 (August 25, 1961), 755-756.

Bungert, Hans. "J. D. Salinger, *The Catcher in the Rye*. Isolation und Kommunikationsversuche des Jugendlichen," *Neueren Sprachen*, No. 5 (May 1960), 208-217. (In German.)

Carpenter, Frederic I. "The Adolescent in American Fiction," *English Journal*, XLVI (September 1957), 313-319.

Corbett, Edward P. J. "Raise High the Barriers, Censors," *America* (November 19, 1960), 441-443.

Costello, Donald P. "The Language of *The Catcher in the Rye*," *American Speech*, XXXIV, 3 (October 1959), 172-181.

Davis, Tom. "J. D. Salinger: 'Some Crazy Cliff' Indeed," *Western Humanities Review*, II (1960), 31-42.

DeGaetano, Madelyn. "An Explication of 'Seymour, an Introduction.'" Unpubl. MA Thesis, Ohio University, 1962.

Didion, Joan. "Finally (Fashionably) Spurious," *The National Review*, XI, 20 (November 18, 1961), 341-342.

Dodge, Stewart. "In Search of 'The Fat Lady,'" *The English Record* (New York State English Council), VIII (Winter 1957), 10-13.

Fiedler, Leslie. "The Eye of Innocence," in *No! In Thunder*. Boston: Beacon Press, 1960. Pp. 251-291.

————. "Up from Adolescence," *Partisan Review*, XXIX, 1 (Winter 1962), 127-131.

Fowler, Albert. "Alien in the Rye," *Modern Age*, I (Fall 1957), 193-197.

Geismar, Maxwell. "J. D. Salinger: The Wise Child and the *New Yorker* School of Fiction," *American Moderns: From Rebellion to Conformity*. New York: Hill and Wang, 1958. Pp. 195-209.

Green, Martin. "Amis and Salinger: The Latitude of Private Conscience," *Chicago Review*, II (Winter 1958), 20-25.

Grunwald, Henry Anatole. "He Touches Something Deep in Us . . . ," *Horizon*, IV, 3 (January 1962), 100-107.

—————. (ed.) *Salinger: A Critical and Personal Portrait*. New York: Harper & Brothers, 1962.

Gutwillig, Robert. "Everybody's Caught 'The Catcher in the Rye,'" *New York Times Book Review, Paperback Section* (January 15, 1961), 38-39.

Gwynn, Frederick L., and Joseph L. Blotner. *The Fiction of J. D. Salinger*. Pittsburgh: University of Pittsburgh Press, 1958.

Hassan, Ihab H. "Rare Quixotic Gesture: The Fiction of J. D. Salinger," *Western Review*, XXI (Summer 1957), 261-280. Reprinted in *Radical Innocence: Studies in the Contemporary Novel*. Princeton, N. J.: Princeton University Press, 1961. Pp. 259-289.

Heiserman, Arthur, and James E. Miller, Jr. "J. D. Salinger: Some Crazy Cliff," *Western Humanities Review*, X (Spring 1956), 129-137.

Hermann, John, "J. D. Salinger: Hello Hello Hello," *College English*, XXII, 4 (January 1961), 262-264.

Hicks, Granville. "J. D. Salinger: Search for Wisdom," *Saturday Review*, XLII, 30 (July 25, 1959), 13, 30.

—————. "Sisters, Sons, and Lovers," *Saturday Review*, XLIV (September 16, 1961), 26.

Jacobs, Robert G. "J. D. Salinger's *The Catcher in the Rye*:

NOTES

NOTES

Holden Caulfield's 'Goddam Autobiography,' " *Iowa English Yearbook* (Fall 1959), 9-14.

Jacobsen, Josephine. "Beautific Signals: The Felicity of J. D. Salinger," *Commonweal*, LXXI, 22 (February 26, 1960), 589-591.

Kaplan, Charles. "Holden and Huck: The Odysseys of Youth," *College English*, XVIII (November 1956), 76-80.

Kapp, Isa. "Salinger's Easy Victory," *The New Leader*, XLV, 1 (January 8, 1962), 27-28.

Kazin, Alfred. "J. D. Salinger: 'Everybody's Favorite,' " *The Atlantic*, CCVIII, 2 (August 1961), 27-31.

Kegel, Charles H. "Incommunicability in Salinger, *The Catcher in the Rye*," *Western Humanities Review*, XI (Spring 1957), 188-190.

Krim, Seymour. "Surface and Substance in a Major Talent," *Commonweal*, LVIII, 3 (April 24, 1953), 78.

———. "Stung by an Exquisite Gadfly," *Washington Post* (September 17, 1961).

Leitch, David. "The Salinger Myth," *Twentieth Century*, CLXVIII, 1005 (November 1960), 428-435.

Levine, Paul. "J. D. Salinger: The Development of the Misfit Hero," *Twentieth Century Literature*, IV, 3 (October 1958), 92-99.

Light, James F. "Salinger's *The Catcher in the Rye*," *Explicator*, XVIII, 9 (June 1960), Item 59.

Maclean, Hugh. "Conservatism in Modern American Fiction," *College English*, XV (March 1954), 315-325.

Marks, Barry A. "Holden in the Rye," *College English*, XXIII, 6 (March 1962), 507.

Marple, Anne. "Salinger's Oasis of Innocence," *New Republic*, CXLV, 12 (September 18, 1961), 22-23.

Martin, Dexter. "Holden in the Rye," *College English*, XXIII, 6 (March 1962), 507-508.

Matthews, James F. "J. D. Salinger: An Appraisal," *University of Virginia Magazine*, I (Spring 1956), 52-60.

Mizener, Arthur. "The Love Song of J. D. Salinger," *Harper's Magazine*, CCXVIII, 1305 (February 1959), 83-90.

Oldsey, Bernard S. "The Movies in the Rye," *College English*, XXIII, 3 (December 1961), 209-215.

Parker, Christopher. "Why the Hell *Not* Smash All the Windows," in Grunwald, *Salinger: A Critical and Personal Portrait* (q.v.), pp. 254-258.

Reiman, Donald H. "Holden in the Rye," *College English*, XXIII, 6 (March 1962), 507.

Seng, Peter J. "The Fallen Idol: The Immature World of Holden Caulfield," *College English*, XXIII, 3 (December 1961), 203-209.

Skow, John. "Sonny: An Introduction," *Time*, LXXVIII (September 15, 1961), 84-86-90.

Steiner, George. "The Salinger Industry," *Nation* (November 14, 1959), 360-363.

Stevenson, David L. "J. D. Salinger: The Mirror of Crisis," *Nation* (March 9, 1957), 215-217.

Updike, John. "Anxious Days for the Glass Family," *New York Times Book Review* (September 17, 1961), 1, 52.

Wakefield, Dan. "Salinger and the Search for Love," *New World Writing #14*. New York: New American Library, 1958. Pp. 68-85.

Wells, Arvin R. "Huck Finn and Holden Caulfield: The Situation of the Hero," *The Ohio University Review*, II (1960), 31-42.

Wiegand, William. "J. D. Salinger: Seventy-Eight Bananas," *Chicago Review*, II (Winter 1958), 3-19.

―――――. "The Knighthood of J. D. Salinger," *New Republic*, CXLI, 16 (October 19, 1959), 19-21.

NOTES

NOTES

WARNER MEMORIAL LIBRARY
EASTERN COLLEGE
ST. DAVIDS, PA. 19087